GOD'S GOT AN ANSWER FOR THAT

JON NAPPA

HARVEST HOUSE PUBLISHERS
EUGENE, OREGON

All Scripture quotations are taken from the Holy Bible, New International Version®, NIV®. Copyright © 1973, 1978, 1984, 2011 by Biblica, Inc.® Used by permission. All rights reserved worldwide.

Cover by Harvest House Publishers, Eugene, Oregon

Julianne Nappa, researcher

The Super Snoopers Logo is a Registered Trademark of Nappa Intellectual Properties, Inc.

GOD'S GOT AN ANSWER FOR THAT

Copyright © 2015 Jon Nappa
Published by Harvest House Publishers
Eugene, Oregon 97402
www.harvesthousepublishers.com

ISBN 978-0-7369-5985-8 (pbk.)

Library of Congress Cataloging-in-Publication Data
    Nappa, Jon, 1958-
    God's got an answer for that / Jon Nappa.
        pages cm
    Includes index.
    1. Christian life—Biblical teaching—Juvenile literature. 2. Conduct of life—Biblical teaching—Juvenile literature. I. Title.
    BV4571.3.N37 2014
    248.8'2—dc23
                                                            2014020270

Printed in China

14 15 16 17 18 19 20 21 22 / RDS-JH / 10 9 8 7 6 5 4 3 2 1

Contents

How to Use This Book

I'm Burt!

I'm Squirt!

Hi! We're the Super Snoopers! We're brothers who find antidotes for life's problems in God's Word.

We know life isn't always easy and kids run into lots of problems along the way. But guess what! For every problem, God's Word has an answer. You just have to know how to find it.

The Bible is a big book with 66 shorter books inside it. Each book may have several chapters, and each chapter has lots of verses. But don't be overwhelmed! This handbook will help you learn where to look. It's like a key to help you unlock the greatest treasure of all— God's Word.

You can become a Truth Sleuth like us by looking at the problems you face every day and snooping out the exact Word from God to help you. (See sample on next page.) Once you've found the right Scripture, you'll know what God says about the question you have or the problem you're facing. When you look up a verse in your Bible, highlight it or underline it. You can write a note to yourself in the margin about how that Word from God helped you.

It makes sense to learn where to look, and that's what being a Truth Sleuth is all about.

I Don't Feel Good About Myself

Problem	Antidote	Word

1 I'm too young. → I will remember everyone is important. → Don't let anyone look down on you because you are young, but set an example for the believers in speech, in conduct, in love, in faith and in purity.

1 Timothy 4:12

2 I'm not smart enough. → I will pray for wisdom. → If any of you lacks wisdom, you should ask God, who gives generously to all without finding fault, and it will be given to you.

James 1:5

3 I just can't do it. → I will remember that I am an overcomer. → For we are God's handiwork, created in Christ Jesus to do good works, which God prepared in advance for us to do.

Ephesians 2:10

Part 1

Help for Every Day from God's Word

In the first section of this book, we'll look at a lot of the situations you'll face as you grow up. Maybe you're getting into a lot of arguments, or maybe you're having trouble obeying your parents. In each situation, we'll ask, "What's the *real* problem?" After we've identified the root of the issue, we'll snoop into God's Word to find an answer for the problem!

Problem

Look for this picture to figure out the real issue that's causing the **problem**.

Antidote

When you see this picture, look for the **antidote** that will show you what to do next.

Word

The picture of the Bible shows you it's time to open up God's **Word**!

Just remember—**p**roblem, **a**ntidote, **w**ord! We're looking in the Bible for **PAW** prints! You don't need to read all these chapters at once, and you don't need to read them in order. You get to pick the chapter that sounds most interesting and important to you.

You can write in this book too! You'll find lots of places to talk about how you're feeling and what you're learning. Putting these feelings in words can help you think them through. It will also be a good book to keep. Later (next week, next year, or even when you're much older), you can come back to this book and remember what you learned.

I Don't Feel Good About Myself

Problem

Antidote

Word

HOLY BIBLE

I'm too young.

I will remember everyone is important.

Don't let anyone look down on you because you are young, but set an example for the believers in speech, in conduct, in love, in faith and in purity.

1 Timothy 4:12

I'm not smart enough.

I will pray for wisdom.

If any of you lacks wisdom, you should ask God, who gives generously to all without finding fault, and it will be given to you.

James 1:5

I just can't do it.

I will remember that I am an overcomer.

For we are God's handiwork, created in Christ Jesus to do good works, which God prepared in advance for us to do.

Ephesians 2:10

Losing confidence or hope is a form of being discouraged. When you start believing your work isn't worth the effort or if you become afraid to try again, you may miss the good things that are just around the corner.

When you dare to try again or are willing to face your doubts and make a second effort, you are demonstrating faith, belief, bravery, and courage.

I felt good about myself when

I did good

From now on, when I don't feel good about myself I will

Read the Bible

I Am Unhappy

Problem	Antidote	Word

Someone was mean to me.

I will pray for them.

Bless those who curse you, pray for those who mistreat you.

Luke 6:28

I can't do what I want.

I will let God know how I feel.

In every situation, by prayer and petition, with thanksgiving, present your requests to God. And the peace of God, which transcends all understanding, will guard your hearts and your minds in Christ Jesus.

Philippians 4:6-7

I didn't get something I wanted.

I will think about what's really important.

Set your minds on things above, not on earthly things.

Colossians 3:1-2

Sometimes you don't feel happy. You think you might want to cry or hide somewhere alone. Many things can cause sadness but they usually have one thing in common—something happened that you didn't want to happen, or something didn't happen that you wanted to happen. *Disappointment* is another word for this, and it doesn't feel good.

Accepting things you cannot change and trusting that you will still be all right is a secret to gratitude and faith—both of which are good antidotes for sadness. Instead of counting all of the things you don't have, consider all of the things you already have.

I felt happy when

From now on, when I feel unhappy I will

I Am Angry

I heard bad news.

I will trust God's will and plan for my life.

God is our refuge and strength, an ever-present help in trouble.

Psalm 46:1

I was bullied or called a bad name.

I will return good even when others aren't good to me.

Love your enemies and pray for those who persecute you.

Matthew 5:44

Someone ignored me.

I will talk to a trusted friend or adult about my feelings.

Cast your cares on the LORD and he will sustain you; he will never let the righteous be shaken.

Psalm 55:22

Being angry means you have unfriendly feelings toward another person, toward a set of circumstances, or even toward yourself. It usually means you disapprove of something that was done or left undone or something said or left unsaid. Anger wants others to know it is displeased and often scares others away or makes them feel anger too.

Forgiveness and kindness are two good antidotes for anger. Forgiveness chooses to hold nothing against anyone. Everyone makes mistakes. Most of the time, mistakes are done accidentally but sometimes it may be on purpose. Either way, forgiveness cancels the anger and offers kindness in return. Kindness can make people who do something against you think twice before doing any more harm, but even if it doesn't change the behavior of the one who tempted you, kindness and forgiveness help you to stay at peace and to remain positive and productive.

I felt calm when _____

_____

_____

_____

_____

From now on, when I feel angry I will _____

_____

_____

_____

_____

_____

I Brag

Problem

Antidote

Word

Problem	Antidote	Word
I want to feel important.	I will recognize what's *most* important.	He must become greater; I must become less. John 3:30
I want more recognition.	I will be content.	I have learned the secret of being content in any and every situation, whether well fed or hungry, whether living in plenty or in want. Philippians 4:12
I want to be better than others.	I will appreciate each person's value.	The eye cannot say to the hand, "I don't need you!" And the head cannot say to the feet, "I don't need you!" On the contrary, those parts of the body that seem to be weaker are indispensable. 1 Corinthians 12:21-22

Showing off can make you the center of attention. This is usually accomplished by trying to do something impressive or daring in front of an audience with the sole purpose of showing them how good and talented you are. People may admire you more or they may admire you less as a result. It is usually better for others to compliment you rather than for you to compliment yourself.

Humility is a good antidote for showing off. Humility recognizes that it is God's gifts and blessings working through you and inside of you that help you to do well. Doing well is best applied by using your gifts to help or serve others, not to win their admiration and praise.

I didn't brag when
_____
_____
_____
_____
_____

From now on, when I start to show off I will
_____
_____
_____
_____
_____

I Am Selfish

Problem	Antidote	Word
I want something for myself.	I will share generously.	Do good…be rich in good deeds, and…be generous and willing to share. 1 Timothy 6:18
Other people don't deserve what I have.	I will not require anything in return.	Let us do good to all people, especially to those who belong to the family of believers. Galatians 6:10
I don't want my things ruined.	I will seek wisdom.	Do not forget to do good and to share with others, for with such sacrifices God is pleased. Hebrews 13:16

Wanting to have everything for yourself is selfishness. That's what not sharing is all about. When you're selfish, it's you and no one else!

Generosity is a great antidote for not sharing. Generosity enjoys experiencing things with others and allowing them access to the things you are enjoying or that you own or control. It includes things like taking turns or giving up your place so others might participate. When you are generous, you think more about others than yourself.

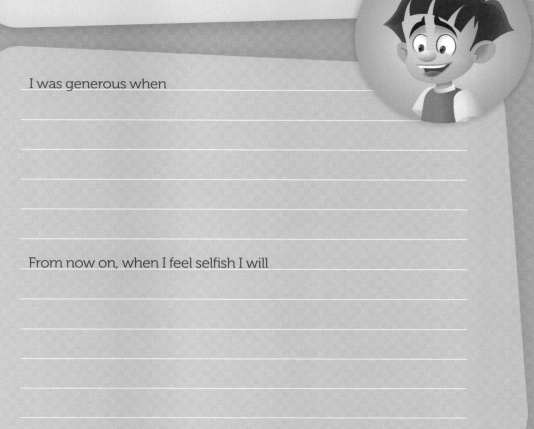

I was generous when
_____
_____
_____
_____
_____

From now on, when I feel selfish I will
_____
_____
_____
_____
_____

I Don't Want to Obey

 Problem

  Antidote

 **Word**

I don't respect my parents.

I will honor my parents.

Children, obey your parents in the Lord, for this is right.

Ephesians 6:1

I don't listen to directions.

I will pay attention to my parents.

A wise son heeds his father's instruction, but a mocker does not respond to rebukes.

Proverbs 13:1

I think I know better than my parents.

I will be humble.

In the same way, you who are younger, submit yourselves to your elders. All of you, clothe yourselves with humility toward one another, because, "God opposes the proud but shows favor to the humble."

1 Peter 5:5

Disobedience happens when you are not paying attention or don't like what you were hearing. You can shut off your ears by not thinking about what others are saying.

Considering the words of others or taking the time to understand what they are trying to say is respectful and wise. It helps to listen by looking at the one who is speaking, thinking about the words they are saying, and even asking questions for help understanding the meaning. Two good antidotes to not listening are focus and attention. Focus aims to think only about what is being said and not allowing your mind to go to other places. Attention means that your eyes and thoughts are directed at the one who is speaking.

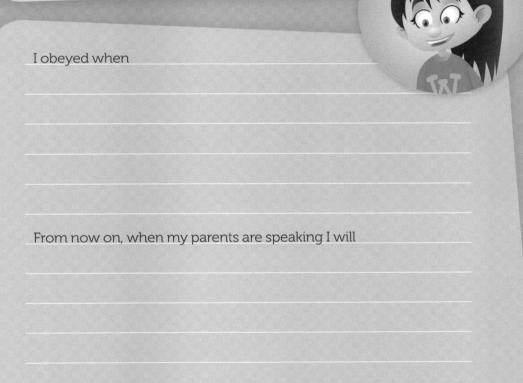

I obeyed when _____

_____

_____

_____

_____

_____

From now on, when my parents are speaking I will _____

_____

_____

_____

_____

_____

_____

I Say Unkind Words

Problem	Antidote	Word
I reacted quickly.	I will think before I speak.	Everyone should be quick to listen, slow to speak and slow to become angry. James 1:19
I was mistreated.	I will return good for evil.	Do not be overcome by evil, but overcome evil with good. Romans 12:21
I'm not in a good mood.	I will be led by the Holy Spirit.	The fruit of the Spirit is love, joy, peace, forbearance, kindness, goodness, faithfulness, gentleness and self-control. Galatians 5:22-23

Speaking harsh or unkind words tears people down and hurts them. Often, you do this when you are feeling hurt too. Unkind words are mean, unfriendly, and don't make people feel good.

Just because a word comes into your mind doesn't mean you have to speak it. Before you open your mouth to speak, ask yourself whether your words will build someone up or tear them down. Choosing words that build up is thoughtful, wise, and good.

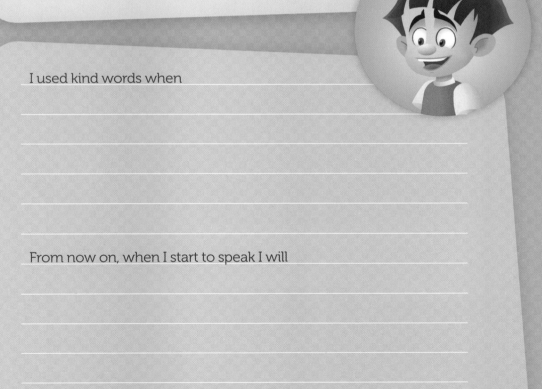

I used kind words when _____
_____
_____
_____
_____
_____

From now on, when I start to speak I will _____
_____
_____
_____
_____
_____

I Am Afraid to Try

Problem

Antidote

Word

Other people are better.

I will trust that God can use even my weakness for His glory.

God chose the foolish things of the world to shame the wise; God chose the weak things of the world to shame the strong.

1 Corinthians 1:27

Other people are watching.

I will be an example of Christ.

The LORD does not look at the things people look at. People look at the outward appearance, but the LORD looks at the heart.

1 Samuel 16:7

It seems too hard.

I will trust God because nothing is impossible with Him.

He who began a good work in you will carry it on to completion.

Philippians 1:6

Feeling shaky or frightened is what being nervous can be like. You usually fear an outcome or result or requirement up ahead. You want to avoid it but feel you can't. The nervousness makes you tremble.

Remembering you are not alone and then going to others for help or advice are two good ways to manage nervousness. Peace is the perfect antidote and comes from resting in God's promises even in the face of troubles. Finding others who share your faith to stand with you also helps to offset the storms. Together you can remind each other of the promises and power of God within.

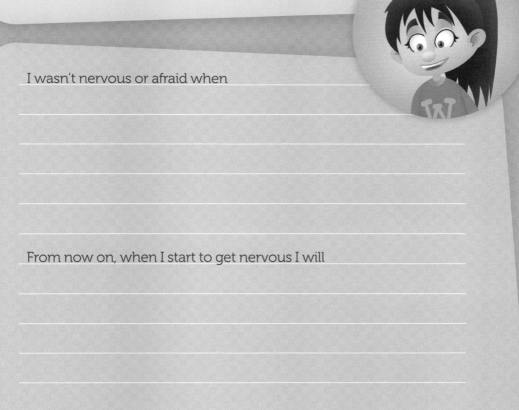

I wasn't nervous or afraid when

_____

_____

_____

_____

From now on, when I start to get nervous I will

_____

_____

_____

_____

I Am Scared

Someone is bullying me.

I will tell an adult I trust.

God is our refuge and strength, an ever-present help in trouble.

Psalm 46:1

I can't do something well.

I will do my best.

May our Lord Jesus Christ himself and God our Father, who loved us and by his grace gave us eternal encouragement and good hope, encourage your hearts and strengthen you in every good deed and word.

2 Thessalonians 2:16-17

I heard bad news.

I will trust God.

[The righteous] will have no fear of bad news; their hearts are steadfast, trusting in the Lord.

Psalm 112:7

Feeling threatened or unsafe are two ways to think about what it's like to be afraid. Someone's actions or words or unfamiliar situations that you don't understand are some of the ways fear can come.

Sometimes fear is a good thing in that it makes you sensible to dangers and reminds you to be careful. Sometimes it can be like a good early warning system to flee a situation and get to a safe place or to others who can help. Other times fear can be due to being uncertain or unclear or unsure. It can feel like you're walking on ice and that your next step might be your last. Finding a safe place and the comforts of safe people is usually the best antidote to such times of fear. If that is impossible to do, remembering that Jesus promised to never leave or forsake you and that you can find a hiding place in His love and promises can be very comforting in times of fear.

I felt brave when

_____

_____

_____

_____

From now on, when I am scared I will

_____

_____

_____

_____

I Didn't Tell the Truth

Problem

Antidote

Word

I didn't want to get into trouble.

I will be responsible for my actions.

An honest witness tells the truth, but a false witness tells lies.

Proverbs 12:17

I wanted to get something.

I will tell the truth even if it hurts.

Keep your tongue from evil and your lips from telling lies.

Psalm 34:13

I lied about someone who hurt me.

I will return good for evil.

Do not repay evil with evil or insult with insult. On the contrary, repay evil with blessing, because to this you were called so that you may inherit a blessing.

1 Peter 3:9

You can come up with reasons for not telling the truth. Sometimes, you fear the truth will get you in trouble. Sometimes you don't want anyone to know the truth because you don't feel good about what the truth is. Other times, you may lie because you don't want to explain.

Being truthful keeps your conscience clear and keeps guilt from finding a place to camp in your heart. However, sometimes it takes courage to speak the truth because it might mean consequences for you. Daring to face the consequences because you love and value the truth is the shortest path to fixing things and turning them around. Otherwise, once a lie is told it usually requires more and more lies to keep up the appearance and such a web of dishonesty entangles you and others. Honesty and trustworthiness are two fine antidotes to lying.

I told the truth when

From now on, when I am tempted to lie I will

I Cheated

Problem: I didn't want to get the answer wrong.

Antidote: I will remember that honesty is more important than getting the right answer.

Word: If we claim to have fellowship with him and yet walk in the darkness, we lie and do not live out the truth.

1 John 1:6

Problem: I didn't want to lose.

Antidote: I will remember that the truth is more important than looking good.

Word: If you do what is right, will you not be accepted? But if you do not do what is right, sin is crouching at your door; it desires to have you, but you must rule over it.

Genesis 4:7

Problem: I wanted more than I was going to get.

Antidote: I will be content with the things I have.

Word: The LORD is my shepherd, I lack nothing.

Psalm 23:1

Secretly breaking the rules is what cheating is all about. You might be tempted to do this when you feel obeying the rules won't get you the results you want. Cheating is often viewed as a shortcut to desirable ends.

Cheating is dishonest and even if you get away with it, it's not a good outcome. You may fool others but you are also fooling yourself. Cheating doesn't allow for the continuing cultivation and growth of good habits, skills, and talents. It will set you up to think you are more capable than you are. Then, when you least expect it, the fact of your cheating will become evident and the embarrassment and failure can be greater than you ever imagined. Playing by the rules, even if it means a lesser outcome than you hoped for, is always the best way to go. In the end, it helps you to improve, grow, and adapt so that, over time, you can get the right results the right way. Then your skills and qualifications are honest and effective and may even benefit others.

I was honest when _____

_____

_____

_____

_____

From now on, when I am tempted to cheat I will _____

_____

_____

_____

_____

_____

I Am Not Happy with What I Have

Problem

Antidote

Word

I am jealous of someone else.

I will be content with what I have.

Keep your lives free from the love of money and be content with what you have, because God has said, "Never will I leave you; never will I forsake you."

Hebrews 13:5

What I have is for someone younger than me.

I will look to help and give to others.

No one should seek their own good, but the good of others.

1 Corinthians 10:24

I always want something new and exciting.

I will appreciate the most important things in life.

If we have food and clothing, we will be content with that.

1 Timothy 6:8

Being unhappy usually means you don't like your circumstances or situation. You want it to be different but it isn't so you are sad.

There are very real situations in life that are not what you most want. Acceptance and patience work well in these cases. Acceptance means you understand your present state to be real and patience means you are willing to be strong enough to wait it out or to work your way out one step at a time. Every moment of life doesn't have to be a party but it can be filled with purpose and effort, faith and trust, patience and love, and other good things.

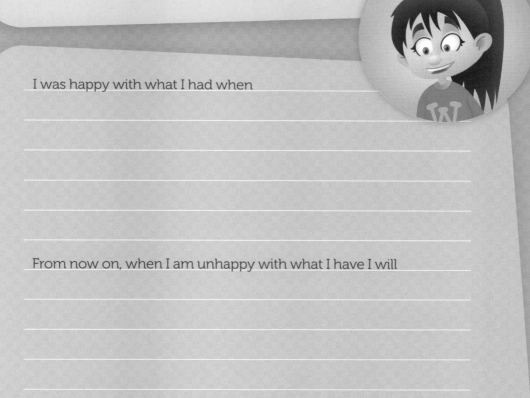

I was happy with what I had when

From now on, when I am unhappy with what I have I will

I Fight with My Brother or Sister

Get rid of all bitterness, rage and anger, brawling and slander, along with every form of malice. Be kind and compassionate to one another, forgiving each other, just as in Christ God forgave you.

Ephesians 4:31-32

We don't understand each other.

I will clear up disagreements.

I keep telling on them.

I will try to work it out before asking for help from parents.

Make every effort to live in peace with everyone and to be holy; without holiness no one will see the Lord.

Hebrews 12:14

They started it.

I will do my best to live peacefully.

If it is possible, as far as it depends on you, live at peace with everyone.

Romans 12:18

Arguments with brothers and sisters can happen over the silliest things. Sometimes you get mad at each other for not sharing or for winning a game or for eating the last chocolate chip cookie. Fighting separates you from each other and causes hurt feelings that don't quickly go away and can make everything else seem like no fun.

Speaking calmly with thoughtful words can make a big difference. Many times it is just a misunderstanding and someone didn't realize how the other person felt about it. Taking the time to work it out peacefully can keep the relationship healthy and fun. This way, you can keep moving forward and enjoy doing other things together.

I didn't start a fight when _____

_____

_____

_____

From now on, when I disagree with my brother or sister I will

_____

_____

_____

_____

I Don't Feel Like Going to Church

Problem

Antidote

Word

Problem	Antidote	Word
I want to stay home.	I will benefit by worshipping with other Christians.	Let us consider how we may spur one another on toward love and good deeds, not giving up meeting together, as some are in the habit of doing, but encouraging one another. Hebrews 10:24-25
None of my friends from school have to go to church.	I will keep a spiritual fervor for the Lord.	Do not conform to the pattern of this world, but be transformed by the renewing of your mind. Romans 12:2
Church isn't any fun.	I will gain spiritual strength from God's Word.	Just as you received Christ Jesus as Lord, continue to live your lives in him, rooted and built up in him, strengthened in the faith as you were taught, and overflowing with thankfulness. Colossians 2:6-7

Once in a while, it may feel easier to sleep in and not get up to go to church. You think you have better things to do than worship God.

It is helpful to remember the benefits of gathering with your church community. Church may not always be as fun as some other activities, but it can be more satisfying and enjoyable when you remember what it does offer. You get to see people who share your faith and you get to join with others to express your appreciation of God. You get to learn more about yourself and your relationship with Jesus. You get to worship and be inspired by thoughts and instructions you might otherwise miss. Thinking of the best parts of church can make your desire to go there become stronger than your desire not to go.

I wanted to go to church when _____

_____

_____

_____

_____

From now on, when I don't want to go to church I will _____

_____

_____

_____

_____

I Don't Help Others

I look out for my own interests.

I will try to achieve my goals and help others with theirs.

In humility value others above yourselves, not looking to your own interests but each of you to the interests of the others.

Philippians 2:3-4

No one helps me.

I will seek to help others as Christ did.

Carry each other's burdens, and in this way you will fulfill the law of Christ.

Galatians 6:2

I don't think about others' feelings.

I will consider others' needs above my own.

Be devoted to one another in love. Honor one another above yourselves.

Romans 12:10

People might need things from you that you don't want to offer. They might need help doing chores or finding something that's missing or locating an answer to a puzzling question. Getting involved means making an effort, and sometimes you don't want to leave whatever comfort you are already experiencing.

Thinking more about what others might need instead of your own self-interests is key to being a good friend and helpful servant. Do you remember reading in the Bible that it is better to give than receive? There is a certain kind of joy and satisfaction that comes from helping others experience what they need and it's different from the kind of enjoyment you get from helping yourself.

I helped others when

_____

_____

_____

_____

From now on, when I don't feel like helping others I will

_____

_____

_____

_____

I Argue with Others

When someone gets angry at me, I get angry back.

I will turn away anger with a soft answer.

A gentle answer turns away wrath, but a harsh word stirs up anger.

Proverbs 15:1

People say things that bother me.

I will avoid foolish arguments.

Don't have anything to do with foolish and stupid arguments, because you know they produce quarrels.

2 Timothy 2:23

I get into arguments when people ask me to do something.

I will shine my light by working without complaining.

Do everything without grumbling or arguing, so that you may become blameless and pure… Then you will shine… like stars in the sky.

Philippians 2:14-15

Yelling and screaming are one way to communicate, and it usually adds a lot of stress and tension to everyone who hears it, including the one who is doing all the shouting. It can also lead to others being loud and angry in return.

A soft word is powerful in the heat of tense and unfriendly arguments. Gentleness can be like a cool rain on a raging fire. Even when tempted to become angry because of what someone else has done or not done, you can choose to not let that emotion rule your tongue. Instead, you can choose to be a wise person who understands how to still a storm with thoughtful words. Take time to be understood and to understand by speaking calmly, carefully, and quietly.

I avoided an argument when _____
_____
_____
_____
_____
_____

From now on, when I start to argue I will _____
_____
_____
_____
_____
_____

I Took Something That Wasn't Mine

Problem

Antidote

Word

I was jealous of something that belonged to someone else.

I will be content with the gifts God has given me.

You shall not covet...anything that belongs to your neighbor.

Exodus 20:17

I wanted something I didn't have.

I will wait or work for the things I want.

Anyone who has been stealing must steal no longer, but must work, doing something useful with their own hands, that they may have something to share with those in need.

Ephesians 4:28

I listened to friends who told me I should steal.

I will care more about God's opinion than the opinions of others.

Do not follow the crowd in doing wrong.

Exodus 23:2

Wanting something you can't have motivates stealing. Either you can't afford it or it's not meant to be available, yet you want it. Taking it without permission and removing it from someone else's possession and making it your own is stealing.

Stealing is robbery. It is being a thief. It is against the commandments of God. Honoring and respecting other people's possessions is the best safeguard against stealing. If you honor someone and respect his or her belongings, you won't take what is theirs. You may ask to borrow something or may accept an invitation to use something of theirs, but an honorable person never takes something from another without permission.

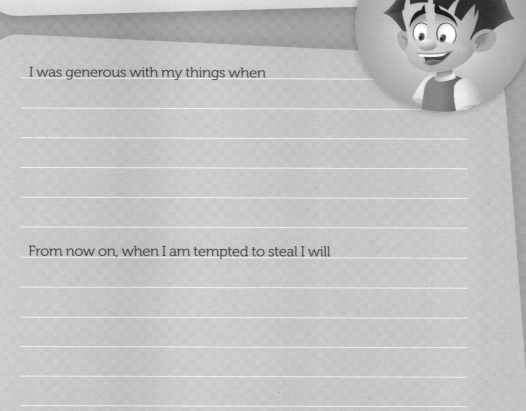

I was generous with my things when _____

_____

_____

_____

_____

_____

From now on, when I am tempted to steal I will _____

_____

_____

_____

_____

_____

I Only Do Things My Way

Problem

Antidote

Word

Problem	Antidote	Word
I don't respect others' opinions.	I will be humble.	All those who exalt themselves will be humbled, and those who humble themselves will be exalted. Luke 14:11
I think my ideas are best.	I will listen to the ideas of others.	Do not be wise in your own eyes; fear the LORD and shun evil. Proverbs 3:7-8
I want to start now.	I will be patient.	If we hope for what we do not yet have, we wait for it patiently. Romans 8:25

It is easy to believe you are right and others are wrong, and sometimes you may be correct to think so. But if you think that way too often, you may become convinced that you are never wrong. Thinking that only you alone know what is best is a dangerous road to travel down. It can lead to huge surprises.

Everyone has something worthwhile to contribute and you can learn from others just as they can learn from you. Take time to consider the counsel of others and then you will be better able to make an informed decision because you've heard good advice.

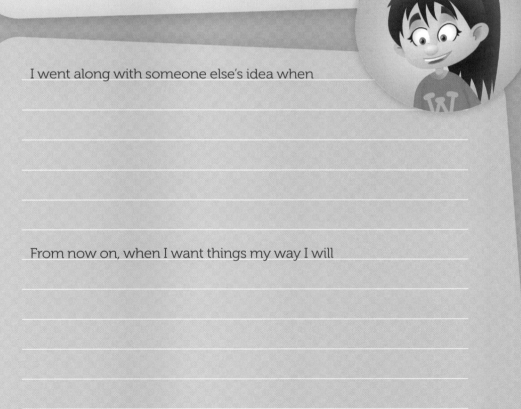

I went along with someone else's idea when

_____

_____

_____

_____

From now on, when I want things my way I will

_____

_____

_____

_____

I Don't Do My Work

Problem

Antidote

Word

I get lazy and put off the work until later.

I will finish the work in front of me so I don't need to worry about it later.

We do not want you to become lazy, but to imitate those who through faith and patience inherit what has been promised.

Hebrews 6:12

I get distracted by other things to do.

I will set aside distractions so I can focus.

You need to persevere so that when you have done the will of God, you will receive what he has promised.

Hebrews 10:36

Work is boring.

I will put my all into whatever I do.

Whatever you do, work at it with all your heart, as working for the Lord, not for human masters.

Colossians 3:23

Not doing work is lazy. Work takes effort and many worthwhile things require hard work. Laziness doesn't like work and accomplishes little or nothing.

Isn't it strange that the more you hang out in bed in the morning, the more tired you become? Have you ever noticed how much more lively you feel once you get up and get going? The same is true with laziness. The lazier you are, the lazier you become. The more you work hard and work well, the more you accomplish and the more enjoyable work becomes. Try it out and see for yourself.

I was proud of my work when

From now on, when I don't feel like working I will

I Don't Want to Go to School

Problem	Antidote	Word

I'm afraid of bullies.

I will talk to a trusted adult and remember that God is my shield.

The LORD is my strength and my shield; my heart trusts in him, and he helps me.

Psalm 28:7

I'm too tired.

I will get to bed on time and wake up ready to learn.

The heart of the discerning acquires knowledge, for the ears of the wise seek it out.

Proverbs 18:15

School is boring.

I will value what God and my teachers want me to learn at this time of my life.

There is a time for everything, and a season for every activity under the heavens.

Ecclesiastes 3:1

Once in a while, it may feel easier to sleep in and not get up to go to school or somewhere else that might not be all fun and games. Not wanting to go somewhere when you are supposed to can cause difficulties for yourself and other people.

It is helpful to remember the benefits of different places and activities. School may not always be exciting, but it's important to spend time learning and growing in knowledge. At this time of your life, school is your job and responsibility—and God is pleased when we do our work well.

I enjoyed school when _____

_____

_____

_____

_____

From now on, when I don't feel like going to school I will _____

_____

_____

_____

_____

_____

I Feel Misunderstood

Problem	**Antidote**	**Word**
Someone judged me.	I will trust that God knows my heart and not worry about the opinions of others.	When they hurled their insults at [Christ], he did not retaliate; when he suffered, he made no threats. Instead, he entrusted himself to him who judges justly. 1 Peter 2:23
I didn't explain.	I will communicate clearly to avoid misunderstandings.	My mouth speaks what is true. Proverbs 8:7
Someone is angry with me.	I will go to them and clear things up.	If you are offering your gift at the altar and there remember that your brother or sister has something against you…first go and be reconciled to them; then come and offer your gift. Matthew 5:23-24

Saying what you mean isn't always easy and sometimes you may not know what to say. People might misunderstand your intentions or actions as a result. Being misunderstood can cause conflict and confusion.

Sometimes you have no choice but to allow people to think what they think even if they misinterpret your intentions or actions. However, it can be worth the effort to explain your actions or ideas to those involved. This means talking it out and helping them to understand what you were trying to do or meant to accomplish and why. This can clear the air and make everyone comfortable again.

I explained my feelings well when _____

_____

_____

_____

_____

From now on, when I don't feel understood I will _____

_____

_____

_____

_____

I Make Fun of People

I don't see other people as important.

I will recognize that God created each person in His image.

So God created mankind in his own image, in the image of God he created them; male and female he created them.

Genesis 1:27

I want to make myself look good by making other people look bad.

I will remember that God's opinion of me is the only one that matters.

All those who exalt themselves will be humbled, and those who humble themselves will be exalted.

Luke 18:14

When I make fun of someone, I'm just saying what everyone else says.

I will look to God's Word to find out how I should act.

Do not be misled: "Bad company corrupts good character." Come back to your senses as you ought, and stop sinning.

1 Corinthians 15:33-34

Sometimes you might feel tempted to say unkind things to people. You might find fault with the way they do things or the way they speak or think or look. Unkind words can hurt people and cause them to lose confidence or to feel poorly about themselves.

If you think about the feelings of others ahead of your own you will be less likely to say hurtful things. If you determine that someone is in need of correction or help, you can choose to find positive and supportive ways to tell him or her. It is possible to offer advice and good counsel in a tone and with words that build people up and help them do well.

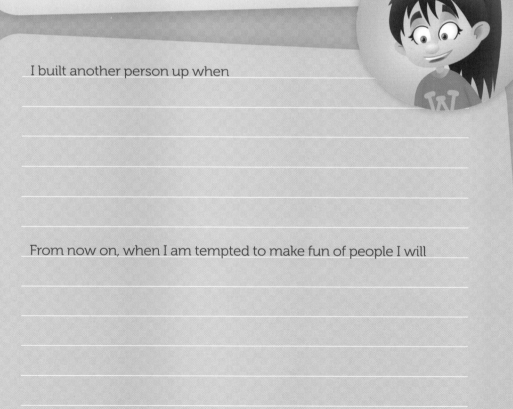

I built another person up when

From now on, when I am tempted to make fun of people I will

I Don't Want to Go to Bed

Problem

Antidote

Word

HOLY BIBLE

Problem	Antidote	Word
I don't like rules.	I will choose to obey.	Children, obey your parents in everything, for this pleases the Lord. Colossians 3:20
I'm scared to be alone in the dark.	I will remember that God will watch over me everywhere I go.	For he will command his angels concerning you to guard you in all your ways. Psalm 91:11
I'm not tired.	I will do each activity at the right time every day.	There is a time for everything, and a season for every activity under the heavens. Ecclesiastes 3:1

Do you ever put up a fight when bedtime rolls around? Is your nighttime ritual a lot of complaining and arguing? If you whine and fuss and don't get to bed on time, you might not be ready for all the next day's activities.

If you don't feel tired, ask your parents if you can read in bed or do another quiet activity before they turn out the lights. Spend some time reflecting on the day. Say a prayer of thanksgiving for all the blessings God sent you, and ask for His help with any difficulties you faced.

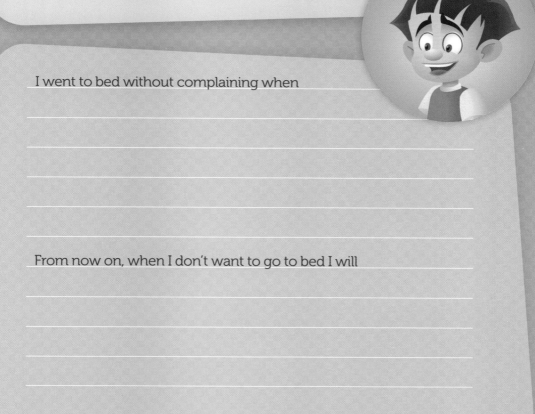

I went to bed without complaining when _____

_____

_____

_____

_____

_____

From now on, when I don't want to go to bed I will _____

_____

_____

_____

_____

_____

I Worry About How I Look

Problem

Antidote

Word

Problem	Antidote	Word
I'm jealous of other people's nice things.	I will be content and take care of the things I own.	Your beauty should not come from outward adornment, such as elaborate hairstyles and the wearing of gold jewelry or fine clothes. Rather, it should be that of your inner self, the unfading beauty of a gentle and quiet spirit, which is of great worth in God's sight. *1 Peter 3:3-4*
I don't think I'm pretty or handsome.	I will remember that I am God's masterpiece.	I praise you because I am fearfully and wonderfully made; your works are wonderful, I know that full well. *Psalm 139:14*
My focus is on the wrong things.	I will look at the needs of others instead of looking in the mirror.	Turn my heart toward your statutes and not toward selfish gain. *Psalm 119:36*

Sometimes you might feel bad about the way you look because you think another person looks better or that people comment on another's appearance but not yours.

It is true that it is wise and good to take care of yourself. You can do this by eating well, washing and bathing when you're supposed to, dressing as nicely as you are able, and grooming yourself in the best way you know how. But you can get it all out of whack if you start worrying about how you look compared to others. What's on the inside is more important than what's on the outside! It's simply not important to look like anyone else, and it doesn't matter whether or not you're the most beautiful or handsome person in the world. It's enough to be the best you can be with whatever you have. Be thankful for it. If physical beauty isn't your best trait you can be confident that something else is. Discover what that is so you can let it shine!

I remembered that I am made in God's image when _____

_____

_____

_____

_____

From now on, when I worry about how I look I will _____

_____

_____

_____

_____

I Have Trouble Waiting

Problem

Antidote

Word

I get bored and don't want to wait my turn.

I will fill my time doing something useful.

But if we hope for what we do not yet have, we wait for it patiently.

Romans 8:25

I'm worried I might miss something if I'm not first.

I will relax and remember that God is in control.

Be completely humble and gentle; be patient, bearing with one another in love.

Ephesians 4:2

I want it now.

I will be patient and wait for the time to come.

Whoever is patient has great understanding, but one who is quick-tempered displays folly.

Proverbs 14:29

Rushing to get something done or not taking the time to finish it can be due to impatience. This often happens when the task at hand is not enjoyable or when there is something else you'd rather be doing and don't want to wait for.

Doing something poorly often means you will have to come back and do it again. Patience helps prevent such unnecessary repetitions by doing it right the first time. Patience endures whatever time it takes to do something properly and completely.

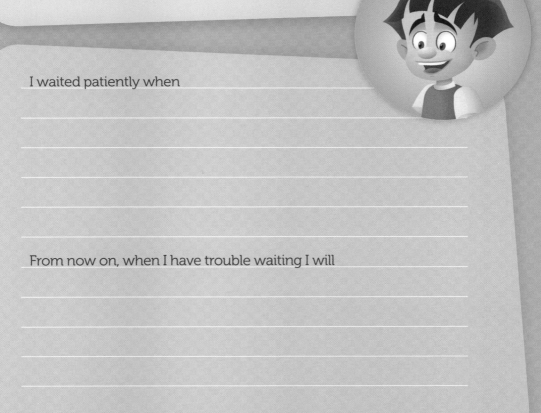

I waited patiently when _____

_____

_____

_____

_____

From now on, when I have trouble waiting I will _____

_____

_____

_____

_____

_____

I Have Doubts About God

Problem

Antidote

Word

I can't feel His presence.

I will remember God is always with me.

Even though I walk through the darkest valley, I will fear no evil, for you are with me; your rod and your staff, they comfort me.

Psalm 23:4

It doesn't seem like He cares.

I will remember that God cares so much He sent Jesus to die for my sins.

For God so loved the world that he gave his one and only Son, that whoever believes in him shall not perish but have eternal life.

John 3:16

My prayers aren't answered.

I will keep asking and seeking God's will.

Ask and it will be given to you; seek and you will find; knock and the door will be opened to you. For everyone who asks receives; the one who seeks finds; and to the one who knocks, the door will be opened.

Luke 11:9-10

It isn't easy trusting something or someone you cannot see.

Faith is trusting something you can't see. Faith for believing in an unseen God comes by hearing the Word of God, which is the Bible. Faith does not demand the evidence of the eyes, but the evidence of the heart. When you read the Bible and learn about God, His love for you, and about His Son Jesus Christ, what do you believe? It's helpful to review His words whenever doubt arrives. You'll discover it strengthens your faith again and again.

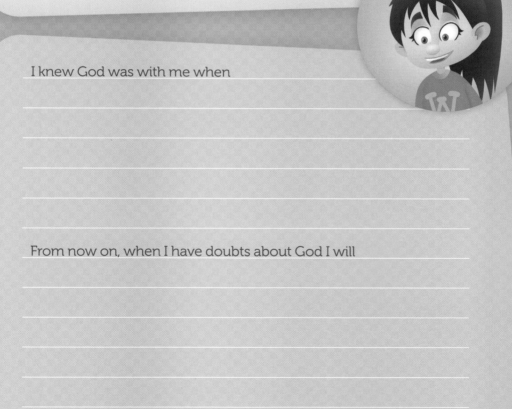

I knew God was with me when _____

_____

_____

_____

_____

_____

From now on, when I have doubts about God I will _____

_____

_____

_____

_____

_____

My Family Is Having Problems

Problem

Antidote

Word

Problem	Antidote	Word
My parents fight a lot.	I will pray for my parents and look for ways to show them I love them.	Honor your father and your mother, as the LORD your God has commanded you, so that you may live long and that it may go well with you in the land the LORD your God is giving you. Deuteronomy 5:16
Someone I love is sick.	I will pray for healing and look for ways to help out around the house.	The LORD sustains them on their sickbed and restores them from their bed of illness. Psalm 41:3
Someone is in trouble.	I will pray for wisdom to help however I can.	In me you may have peace. In this world you will have trouble. But take heart! I have overcome the world. John 16:33

Every family has problems sometimes. Maybe people are fighting, or there's tension over your parents' work, or someone is sick or in trouble.

Jesus told us that we'll always face problems in this world. But there's good news too! God has wisdom for every situation you may find yourself in. God tells us we can work things out with unhappy family members by taking time to communicate. This helps everyone understand what each person is feeling. Together, you will find the way out.

I pray for God to help my family by _____

_____

_____

_____

_____

From now on, when my family is having problems I will _____

_____

_____

_____

_____

I Need to Forgive

Problem	Antidote	Word

Problem

Someone asked me for forgiveness, but it's hard.

Antidote

I can forgive.

Word

Bear with each other and forgive one another if any of you has a grievance against someone. Forgive as the Lord forgave you.

Colossians 3:13

Someone keeps doing bad things.

I will forgive them again.

Peter came to Jesus and asked, "Lord, how many times shall I forgive my brother or sister who sins against me? Up to seven times?" Jesus answered, "I tell you, not seven times, but seventy-seven times."

Matthew 18:21-22

I did something wrong, and I can't stop thinking about it.

I can forgive myself.

Forgetting what is behind and straining toward what is ahead, I press on toward the goal to win the prize for which God has called me heavenward in Christ Jesus.

Philippians 3:13-14

You can have hard feelings toward a person and keep something in your memory that's like a record of wrongs he or she has done to you.

Canceling whatever list of wrongs you attach to a person is what forgiveness is all about. Have you "written a ticket" in your mind accusing a friend of mistreating you? Or lying to you? Or not thinking about you the way he or she should? Have you written lots of tickets charging people with crimes? Forgiveness rips all those tickets up, just like Jesus did when He died on the cross and paid for all of your sins. Love covers over an endless list of wrongs because love forgives. Love the people who have done you wrong and forgive every one of them.

I forgave someone when

From now on, when I don't want to forgive I will

I Didn't Keep My Promise

Problem

Antidote

Word

My promise was too hard to keep.

Even though it's hard, I will keep my promises.

[The one] who keeps an oath even when it hurts...will never be shaken.

Psalm 15:4-5

Someone pressured me into breaking my promise.

I will do what is right in God's eyes instead of caring about the opinions of others.

Be strong in the Lord and in his mighty power. Put on the full armor of God, so that you can take your stand against the devil's schemes.

Ephesians 6:10-11

I shouldn't have made the promise in the first place.

I will be more thoughtful about the promises I make.

It is better not to make a vow than to make one and not fulfill it.

Ecclesiastes 5:5

When you make a promise, you give your word that you will do something—or maybe not do something. The person you make the promise to is putting all their trust in you. If you keep your promise, people will know that you're a person worthy of even more trust.

But sometimes you think you have a good reason for breaking your promise. This takes away the trust people have in you and makes them wonder if you really care about them. Not keeping your promise can cause problems for lots of people. Before you make a promise, ask yourself and God if it's a promise you can keep. If so, ask for God's help with whatever you have to do!

I kept a promise when _____

_____

_____

_____

_____

From now on, when I have trouble keeping a promise I will _____

_____

_____

_____

_____

I Don't Have Any Friends

Problem	Antidote	Word
I am too shy.	I will rely on the power of the Holy Spirit in me.	For the Spirit God gave us does not make us timid, but gives us power, love and self-discipline. 2 Timothy 1:7
I am not friendly.	I will think of how I want others to treat me.	Do to others as you would have them do to you. Luke 6:31
My old friends are ignoring me or bullying me.	I will talk to an adult and trust God to bring me new friends.	One who has unreliable friends soon comes to ruin, but there is a friend who sticks closer than a brother. Proverbs 18:24

Not having friends is lonely.

Sometimes it is good to find a room with just you in it. Solitude can be nice from time to time. It can be good for resting or praying or thinking. But being alone too much can be awful, especially when you see everyone else having fun around you. God promises to set the lonely in families because His children are made to be connected one to another. Having friends means having many places to go to for help or for advice or for laughs or comfort. It also means having others to share and grow and experience things with. Take the time to be a friend and you'll find friends making time to be friendly with you. One way to make more friends is by taking an interest in learning about what others are thinking or feeling or discovering something about their own life story.

I made a friend when _____

_____

_____

_____

_____

_____

From now on, when I feel lonely I will _____

_____

_____

_____

_____

_____

I Don't Feel Thankful

Problem

Antidote

Word

Life is dragging me down.

I will put my hope in God.

In me you may have peace. In this world you will have trouble. But take heart! I have overcome the world.

John 16:33

I didn't get what I wanted.

Regardless of how I feel, I will thank God for who He is.

I will sacrifice a thank offering to you and call on the name of the Lord.

Psalm 116:17

Someone else got what I wanted.

I will celebrate with others who are thankful.

Rejoice with those who rejoice; mourn with those who mourn.

Romans 12:15

Not being thankful means you're unhappy with what you have and unhappy about what you don't have.

Always wanting something new and fresh leads to not valuing what you already have. It also leads to never being satisfied because nothing stays new and fresh forever. You can beat this unhealthy attitude by thinking about the many things you already have and experiencing them again. Take the time to get reacquainted with them, just like you did when you first received them. You can do this with people, places, pets, and other things. You'll be delighted to see how rich it makes you feel.

I felt grateful when

_____

_____

_____

_____

From now on, when I don't feel thankful I will

_____

_____

_____

_____

I Don't Know How to Talk to God

Problem

Antidote

Word

Problem	Antidote	Word
I don't know what to say.	I will talk to God as a friend and father.	The Spirit helps us in our weakness. We do not know what we ought to pray for, but the Spirit himself intercedes for us through wordless groans. *Romans 8:26*
I don't think my prayers matter to God.	I will remember that God loves to hear my prayers.	Do not be anxious about anything, but in every situation, by prayer and petition, with thanksgiving, present your requests to God. *Philippians 4:6*
I've sinned too much for God to pay attention to me.	I know that God has covered my sins with His grace.	If we confess our sins, he is faithful and just and will forgive us our sins and purify us from all unrighteousness. *1 John 1:9*

It can be intimidating to sit down with the Creator of the universe.

God may seem too big to be interested in you but He says you should come boldly into His presence. He invites you to be like a child running to the open arms of a loving parent. He says there is nothing to be afraid of once you've let Christ into your heart. Jesus is the key that unlocks the door to God's presence. He wants you to come and spend time with Him. You can ask Him things, tell Him things, and listen to Him to tell you things. He loves to communicate with all of His children, and that's what all of us are.

I was able to talk to God when

From now on, when I don't know how to talk to God I will

Part 2

Bible Dictionary

A dictionary is a list of words and their meanings. This dictionary does way more than that, so it's got a big name: a *concordance*. That's a fancy way of saying, "Here's where to find something in the Bible." We'll look at what each word means, and then we'll snoop into the Bible to see four different places where God uses it. Whenever you're wondering what God has to say about a certain subject, just flip to those verses!

You might want to start with the last word in this dictionary, *wisdom*, because that's what you'll be collecting. The more you learn about God's Word, the more full of wisdom and understanding you'll be. The world needs more wise people who know what God says.

Bible

The Bible is God's Word for His people. In it you can find true stories about things that happened a long time ago. You can find wisdom and good advice. You can find out all about Jesus. When you read your Bible, you'll learn a lot about God and yourself.

The law from your mouth is more precious to me than thousands of pieces of silver and gold.

Psalm 119:72

Keep this Book of the Law always on your lips; meditate on it day and night, so that you may be careful to do everything written in it. Then you will be prosperous and successful.

Joshua 1:8

All Scripture is God-breathed and is useful for teaching, rebuking, correcting and training in righteousness, so that the servant of God may be thoroughly equipped for every good work.

2 Timothy 3:16-17

I have hidden your word in my heart that I might not sin against you.

Psalm 119:11

Church

Wherever people get together to worship God and learn about Him, that's church! When you gather with others who love Jesus, you can help each other grow in faith and do more for others in the world who need help.

Since you are eager for gifts of the Spirit, try to excel in those that build up the church.

1 Corinthians 14:12

Let us consider how we may spur one another on toward love and good deeds, not giving up meeting together, as some are in the habit of doing, but encouraging one another—and all the more as you see the Day approaching.

Hebrews 10:24-25

Keep watch over yourselves and all the flock of which the Holy Spirit has made you overseers. Be shepherds of the church of God, which he bought with his own blood.

Acts 20:28

Christ loved the church and gave himself up for her to make her holy, cleansing her by the washing with water through the word.

Ephesians 5:25-26

Confession

Confession means telling God when you've done something wrong. God already knows what you've done, but He still wants you to talk to Him about it. When you talk with God about your sins and ask for forgiveness, you'll feel better and know what to do next to make things right.

Confess your sins to each other and pray for each other so that you may be healed. The prayer of a righteous person is powerful and effective.

James 5:16

Have mercy on me, O God, according to your unfailing love; according to your great compassion blot out my transgressions. Wash away all my iniquity and cleanse me from my sin.

Psalm 51:1-2

Then I acknowledged my sin to you and did not cover up my iniquity. I said, "I will confess my transgressions to the LORD." And you forgave the guilt of my sin.

Psalm 32:5

Each of us will give an account of ourselves to God.

Romans 14:12

Eternal Life

Jesus says there's a place for you in heaven if you know Him. We will live there forever with Him!

For God so loved the world that he gave his one and only Son, that whoever believes in him shall not perish but have eternal life.

John 3:16

My Father's house has many rooms; if that were not so, would I have told you that I am going there to prepare a place for you? And if I go and prepare a place for you, I will come back and take you to be with me that you also may be where I am.

John 14:2-3

The Son of God has come and has given us understanding, so that we may know him who is true. And we are in him who is true by being in his Son Jesus Christ. He is the true God and eternal life.

1 John 5:20

This is what he promised us—eternal life.

1 John 2:25

Faith

Faith is belief in God and what He says in the Bible. Even though you can't see God, you can know that He is with you and will help you. When you look at the world around you, you can see that God is at work. Faith is a gift from God and it gives us hope.

The righteous person will live by his faithfulness.

Habakkuk 2:4

If you have faith as small as a mustard seed, you can say to this mountain, "Move from here to there," and it will move. Nothing will be impossible for you.

Matthew 17:20

Without faith it is impossible to please God, because anyone who comes to him must believe that he exists and that he rewards those who earnestly seek him.

Hebrews 11:6

Faith is confidence in what we hope for and assurance about what we do not see.

Hebrews 11:1

Forgiveness

Has someone ever owed you something? When you forgive, it's like saying that person doesn't owe you anything anymore. You don't hold anything against them. God gives us forgiveness for our sins and doesn't ask for anything in return. It's free. All you have to do is ask for it. You can give forgiveness to others too.

Blessed is the one whose transgressions are forgiven, whose sins are covered.

Psalm 32:1

If you forgive anyone's sins, their sins are forgiven; if you do not forgive them, they are not forgiven.

John 20:23

Therefore, I tell you, her many sins have been forgiven—as her great love has shown. But whoever has been forgiven little loves little.

Luke 7:47

As far as the east is from the west, so far has he removed our transgressions from us.

Psalm 103:12

Grace

Grace comes from God and from other people. Grace is forgiveness and love when we don't deserve it. God gives grace freely if we're willing to take it. It's a gift.

Grace and truth came through Jesus Christ.

John 1:17

For God so loved the world that he gave his one and only Son, that whoever believes in him shall not perish but have eternal life.

John 3:16

My grace is sufficient for you, for my power is made perfect in weakness.

2 Corinthians 12:9

It is by grace you have been saved.

Ephesians 2:5

Honesty

Honesty doesn't hide anything. It means that you tell the truth and mean it. Sometimes it's hard to be honest, but it's always the right thing to do. The Bible is full of honest truth, the kind that never changes, whether others believe it or not.

An honest witness tells the truth, but a false witness tells lies.

Proverbs 12:17

Truthful lips endure forever, but a lying tongue lasts only a moment.

Proverbs 12:19

Let us not love with words or speech but with actions and in truth.

1 John 3:18

An honest answer is like a kiss on the lips.

Proverbs 24:26

Hope

Hope is looking forward to good things, trusting that they will happen. Hope is when you trust God because He knows best. God's promises also give lots of hope. He says He will always take care of you. He also says He has a place ready for you in heaven. What a great thing to hope for!

Be joyful in hope, patient in affliction, faithful in prayer.

Romans 12:12

"For I know the plans I have for you," declares the Lord, "plans to prosper you and not to harm you, plans to give you hope and a future."

Jeremiah 29:11

For in this hope we were saved. But hope that is seen is no hope at all. Who hopes for what they already have? But if we hope for what we do not yet have, we wait for it patiently.

Romans 8:24-25

On him we have set our hope.

2 Corinthians 1:10

Joy

Joy is different from being happy. You can be happy when you get lots of presents on your birthday. But happiness can disappear when your new toy breaks or a friend gets mad at you. Joy is bigger than being happy. It's a good feeling, but it's also knowing that God loves you no matter what. Joy is something that isn't changed by what is happening around you.

The joy of the LORD is your strength.

Nehemiah 8:10

Come, let us sing for joy to the LORD; let us shout aloud to the Rock of our salvation.

Psalm 95:1

Those who sow with tears will reap with songs of joy. Those who go out weeping, carrying seed to sow, will return with songs of joy, carrying sheaves with them.

Psalm 126:5-6

You will fill me with joy in your presence.

Psalm 16:11

Love

Love is a deep and unchanging feeling toward another. It means that you consider them most important and will take care of them and do good things for them.

Love comes from God.

1 John 4:7

Love the Lord your God with all your heart and with all your soul and with all your mind and with all your strength.

Mark 12:30

And now these three remain: faith, hope and love. But the greatest of these is love.

1 Corinthians 13:13

Anyone who loves God must also love their brother and sister.

1 John 4:21

Obedience

Obedience means that you do what you're asked to do without arguing. Lots of people ask you to do things—your mom and dad, your teacher, your brothers and sisters, your friends, and the government. God asks you to do things too. Learning to obey is part of growing up. When you obey, others know they can trust you.

Now if you obey me fully and keep my covenant, then out of all nations you will be my treasured possession.

Exodus 19:5

Faithfully obey the commands I am giving you today—to love the LORD your God and to serve him with all your heart and with all your soul.

Deuteronomy 11:13

Be careful to obey all these regulations I am giving you, so that it may always go well with you and your children after you, because you will be doing what is good and right in the eyes of the LORD your God.

Deuteronomy 12:28

Children, obey your parents in everything, for this pleases the Lord.

Colossians 3:20

Praise

Praise is when you look for all the good in someone and tell them about it. God deserves our praise because He does so many good things.

I will extol the LORD at all times; his praise will always be on my lips.

Psalm 34:1

I praise you because I am fearfully and wonderfully made; your works are wonderful, I know that full well.

Psalm 139:14

The heavens praise your wonders, LORD, your faithfulness too.

Psalm 89:5

Let everything that has breath praise the LORD. Praise the LORD.

Psalm 150:6

Prayer

Prayer is talking to God. We may thank Him, worship Him, ask Him for help, tell Him we love Him, or just listen to Him—it's all prayer. Prayer is a gift from God. He hears our prayers and answers them.

Bless those who curse you, pray for those who mistreat you.

Luke 6:28

Is anyone among you in trouble? Let them pray. Is anyone happy? Let them sing songs of praise.

James 5:13

The Spirit helps us in our weakness. We do not know what we ought to pray for, but the Spirit himself intercedes for us through wordless groans.

Romans 8:26

The prayer of a righteous person is powerful and effective.

James 5:16

Promises

A promise means you'll do what you say, no matter what. A promise is a serious thing and isn't meant to be broken. When God makes a promise, He keeps His word.

My eyes stay open through the watches of the night, that I may meditate on your promises.

Psalm 119:148

I am with you and will watch over you wherever you go, and I will bring you back to this land. I will not leave you until I have done what I have promised you.

Genesis 28:15

He has given us his very great and precious promises, so that through them you may participate in the divine nature.

2 Peter 1:4

Let us hold unswervingly to the hope we profess, for he who promised is faithful.

Hebrews 10:23

Purity

Purity is being clean and simple. Being pure is filling your mind with so many good things that there's no room for the bad stuff.

Blessed are the pure in heart, for they will see God.

Matthew 5:8

Whatever is true, whatever is noble, whatever is right, whatever is pure, whatever is lovely, whatever is admirable— if anything is excellent or praiseworthy—think about such things.

Philippians 4:8

To the pure, all things are pure, but to those who are corrupted and do not believe, nothing is pure. In fact, both their minds and consciences are corrupted.

Titus 1:15

Don't let anyone look down on you because you are young, but set an example for the believers in speech, in conduct, in love, in faith and in purity.

1 Timothy 4:12

Sadness

Sadness is the opposite of happiness. Sometimes you cry; sometimes your throat or your stomach hurts. *Sorrow* and *grief* are two words that also mean sadness.

But you, God, see the trouble of the afflicted; you consider their grief and take it in hand.

Psalm 10:14

Be merciful to me, LORD, for I am in distress; my eyes grow weak with sorrow, my soul and body with grief.

Psalm 31:9

Very truly I tell you, you will weep and mourn while the world rejoices. You will grieve, but your grief will turn to joy.

John 16:20

The LORD will be your everlasting light, and your days of sorrow will end.

Isaiah 60:20

Sin

Sin is anything you think, do, or say that doesn't please God. Sin separates us from God, but the blood of Jesus washes us clean.

All have sinned and fall short of the glory of God.

Romans 3:23

Against you, you only, have I sinned and done what is evil in your sight; so you are right in your verdict and justified when you judge.

Psalm 51:3-4

If we confess our sins, he is faithful and just and will forgive us our sins and purify us from all unrighteousness.

1 John 1:9

God demonstrates his own love for us in this: While we were still sinners, Christ died for us.

Romans 5:8

Submission

Submission is letting those who love you be your boss. When you submit to God by doing what He asks, you let Him be the boss of you. It doesn't sound like much fun, but when you submit to God, things are actually a lot easier! God helps you make good choices and helps you find joy, even when you have to do hard things.

Submit to one another out of reverence for Christ.

Ephesians 5:21

Let everyone be subject to the governing authorities, for there is no authority except that which God has established. The authorities that exist have been established by God.

Romans 13:1

Have confidence in your leaders and submit to their authority, because they keep watch over you as those who must give an account. Do this so that their work will be a joy, not a burden, for that would be of no benefit to you.

Hebrews 13:17

Submit yourselves, then, to God.

James 4:7

Truth

Truth is fact. Truth is honest. Truth is what is real. God has told us lots of truth in His Word, the Bible. For instance, it's always true that He loves us and will never leave us.

Kings take pleasure in honest lips; they value the one who speaks what is right.

Proverbs 16:13

Jesus said, "If you hold to my teaching, you are really my disciples. Then you will know the truth, and the truth will set you free."

John 8:31-32

Jesus answered, "I am the way and the truth and the life. No one comes to the Father except through me."

John 14:6

Speak the truth to each other, and render true and sound judgment.

Zechariah 8:16

Wisdom

Wisdom means a lot more than knowing things. It's making good choices and thinking things through. Wisdom is doing what's right and listening to good advice. Being smart is good; being wise is even better!

To God belong wisdom and power; counsel and understanding are his.

Job 12:13

The fear of the LORD is the beginning of wisdom; all who follow his precepts have good understanding.

Psalm 111:10

Get wisdom, get understanding; do not forget my words or turn away from them.

Proverbs 4:5

Listen, my sons, to a father's instruction; pay attention and gain understanding.

Proverbs 4:1

Burt and Squirt want you!

Discover the world of the Super Snoopers and become a Truth Sleuth yourself!

Ask your mom and dad to join you and visit www.thesupersnoopers.com

You'll find games, stories, comics, and more ways to snoop into God's Word.

And don't miss...

God's Got an Answer for That!
Devotional

God's Got an Answer for That!
Activity Book